STEAM TUGS
A Colour Portfolio

David L. Williams

Introduction

Once a familiar sight in every major and minor port in the United Kingdom, steam tugs were among the very earliest applications of mechanical propulsion to marine craft. The *Charlotte Dundas*, an experimental stern-wheeler steamboat designed by Robert Symington and completed in 1801, may be regarded as the very first powered tug. Designed to replace horses, then the only means of pulling barges along the inland waterways, in March 1802 she demonstrated the extraordinary power potential of steam-driven vessels when she towed two loaded barges non-stop along the length of the Firth & Clyde Canal, a distance of some 20 miles. Though successful, the *Charlotte Dundas* did not remain in service, because the canal's owners feared that the wash generated by her paddles would erode the banks. Nevertheless, it was not long before steam tugs, towing both ships and dumb barges, became commonplace around the country.

Perhaps the most enduring image of an early steam tug is that showing the fighting *Temeraire* being towed to Beatson's ship-breaking yard at Rotherhithe in the painting by Joseph Mallord William Turner, a canvas dating from 1839. The tug depicted is the *Monarch*, the pioneer craft of William Watkins, one of the earliest commercial towage concerns, established in 1833. Another early

Watkins tug which achieved distinction was the *Anglia*, which in 1878 towed the obelisk Cleopatra's Needle part of the way from Egypt to the River Thames.

The steam tug remained dominant for almost a century and a half, originally fitted with paddle wheels and then, from around the 1870s, driven by screw propellers. Screw-propelled tugs had the benefit of greater power because their propellers were completely immersed, providing more efficient thrust. In contrast, paddle-propelled tugs were more manœuvrable, particularly those that had independent drive to each paddle wheel — an important requirement for those working in the confined spaces and shallow waters between quays and piers. The installation of Kort nozzles eventually gave screw-propelled tugs a degree of manœuvrability comparable with their paddle counterparts.

From the 19th century through to the end of the steam-tug era, the engines installed aboard these craft reflected the continuing developments that were taking place in marine engineering. The older paddle tugs generally had either side-lever or 'grasshopper' engines, or diagonal engines arranged with one, two or three cylinders driving the paddle shaft.

Previous page: Built in 1935 by A. Hall & Co, Aberdeen, for Gamecock Tugs, London, the *Crested Cock* (177grt, 96ft) is seen here wearing Gamecock colours as she arrives at the Royal Terrace Pier. Gamecock Tugs Ltd was originally formed *c*1880 by a group of Thames river pilots aiming to break the monopoly then held by the William Watkins towage business. Along with the *Atlantic Cock*, the *Crested Cock* was broken up at Antwerp in 1970.

First published 2002

ISBN 0 7110 2857 5

© Ian Allan Publishing Ltd 2002

Published by Ian Allan Publishing

an imprint of Ian Allan Publishing Ltd, Hersham, Surrey KT12 4RG.
Printed by Ian Allan Printing Ltd, Hersham, Surrey KT12 4RG.

Code: 0207/B2

The inverted steam reciprocating engine, with its cylinders arranged vertically over the crankshaft — the final form of the marine reciprocating engine — was introduced around the middle of the 19th century, initially in 'simple' or single-expansion form. As higher boiler pressures were achieved, 'compound' or double-expansion engines were developed from the early 1860s, followed from 1875 by triple-expansion engines, combining high and low pressure cylinders. Within a very few years of their introduction, triple-expansion marine engines had reached a remarkably high degree of efficiency. The screw steam tugs that entered service during the period from the late 19th century through to just prior to World War 1 were mostly fitted with compound expansion engines. All the other screw steam tugs built from that time were fitted with triple-expansion machinery producing much-increased power output. Quadruple-expansion power-plants — representing the ultimate development of the steam reciprocating marine engine — were never fitted to tugs because of the extreme size of these installations. Steam turbine engines, being unsuitable for use on towage craft, were never installed either.

A quarter of a century or so ago, steam tugs were completely superseded by diesel-engined towage craft. With turn-key ignition, motor vessels offered ready operational availability at any time, whereas their steam-driven counterparts either needed time to raise steam or had to be kept in steam for long periods — an expensive business if there were no ships to handle or no river traffic to move.

The only Admiralty tug of her type, the *Pert* (1,023 tons full-load displacement, 179ft 6in) was also the largest paddle tug to serve the Senior Service, with a bollard pull of 20 tons and double-expansion steam engines producing 2,000ihp. She was built by John I. Thornycroft and launched at Woolston on 5 April 1916. Because of her great size, the *Pert* (Pennant No W42) made an ideal VIP-passenger carrier during Fleet Reviews and fulfilled this function at many such grand occasions, including the Coronation Review of 1953. Throughout her life, she worked handling naval ships at Plymouth, Portsmouth and Devonport, where this photograph was taken in the summer of 1961. Later that year, in October, after a long and valuable career, she was withdrawn from service. She went for scrap at Rysdijk, in the Netherlands, in June 1962. Alongside her in this view is the Admiralty twin-screw motor tug *Accord* (641grt), completed in 1958. *R. C. Riley*

Although diesel tugs were introduced from the late 1940s, most notably on the inland waterways, steam tugs continued to be built for another 10 years or so, though with boilers that were oil-fired rather than coal-fired. However, many of these final steam-powered tugs subsequently had their engines converted to internal combustion.

All the photographs in this album were taken towards the end of the steam-tug era, from the mid-1950s through to the late 1960s and early 1970s — a time when the pace at which diesel tugs were taking over was fast accelerating. This was a period of other changes to the towage business, too. The few paddle tugs that still remained in service were being rapidly phased out, although, as an interesting reversal of this trend, the Admiralty commissioned a new class of paddle tugs late in the 1950s, albeit all diesel-engined.

Competitive pressures were precipitating mergers and working alliances between the tug-operating companies. Consequently this was also a period that witnessed the adoption of many changes in company liveries as the various changes of ownership occurred.

In 1949 three Thames towage concerns — Elliott Steam Tugs (formed in 1879), William Watkins and Gamecock Tugs (dating from 1880) — formed Ship Towage (London). Each constituent company in the group initially retained its original colour scheme but, from the mid-1960s, new colours were adopted, the elements of which were drawn from all the earlier schemes. W. H. J. Alexander (founded in 1883 and better known as Sun Tugs) joined the consortium in 1969, when it was reconstituted as London Tugs Ltd. Six years later, all four companies disappeared completely as independent concerns when Alexandra Towing, which had originated in Liverpool in 1887 and then expanded to Southampton and Swansea in the 1920s, took over London Tugs.

It was a similar story on the River Tyne, where France Fenwick (the largest towage fleet on the North East coast since 1918), Lawson-Batey and Ridley Tugs (one of the oldest Tyne towage concerns, dating from the 1840s) joined forces as Tyne Tugs in the late 1950s, adopting a universal style of colouring which was rather less attractive than any of the three schemes that it replaced.

Perhaps the most voracious of the towage companies, whose aggressive expansion policy gradually swallowed up the majority of the independent operators on the rivers Mersey and Thames, was the Alexandra Towing Co. In 1966 it absorbed Liverpool Screw Towing & Lighterage (founded in 1877), along with its subsidiary, North West Tugs. Two years later it took over J. H. Lamey Ltd, a concern which had been established in 1916. Alexandra Towing's biggest coup was its 1975 acquisition of the complete London Tugs group.

The majority of the pictures in this album depict ship-handling or harbour tugs — vessels of a compromise design which normally operated within the confines of ports. Combining a short hull, of around 100ft, with sturdy construction, they generally had sufficiently powerful engines to permit them to work in open sea conditions, if required. They had a bollard pull (ie the maximum weight a tug can safely tow) in the range of 4 to 15 tons.

A derivative of the steam ship-handling tug, of which a few examples are shown here, was the tender tug, which performed normal tug duties but which was also fitted with substantial accommodation for transferring passengers between the docks and ocean liners that did not enter port. With a longer and, usually, beamier hull, their greater capacity was reflected in their much higher gross tonnage measurement.

In these pages too are examples of smaller steam-powered craft-handling or river tugs, used for hauling lighters, and even smaller steam tenders, at the bottom end of the scale. The only type not represented is their complete opposite — the large, commercial ocean-going tug, employed on deep-ocean salvage work and long-distance tows. The latter were much longer and larger, and had a considerably more powerful bollard-pull capability than their ship-handling counterparts. Typically, the bollard pull of craft-handling tugs was between 2 and 7 tons; by comparison, ocean-going tugs were capable of pulling loads of between 12 and 40 tons.

Admiralty steam tugs of the Royal Navy, Dockyard Directorate and, later, the Port Auxiliary Service performed broadly the same roles as commercial towage vessels but were designated rather differently. The equivalent of ocean-going tugs are naval Fleet tugs, which are painted grey. Dockyard tugs are the type used for handling Royal Navy ships in port. They are distinguished by their black hulls and yellow-brown funnels with black tops and narrow blue band. Some photographs of steam-powered versions of dockyard tugs are shown in the pages that follow.

Apart from a small number of exceptions (each of which is annotated), all of the photographs presented here were taken by Kenneth Wightman, a noted steam enthusiast and a proficient amateur photographer who concentrated initially on railway subjects and then on shipping of all types. Armed with his trusted Leica camera and cassettes of the ground-breaking Kodachrome transparency film (the first truly viable integral tri-pack colour film produced by Kodak for amateur use, offering superb colour rendition), he set about making this unique record. Thus, this book is a celebration of both the twilight era of British steam tugs and of the colour photography of Kenneth Wightman, besides showing some of the classic British merchant ships of that era that were also caught on camera.

Kenneth Wightman was a lifelong resident of Beckenham, Kent. He was educated at Dulwich College before he was called up for service with the Army in 1939, joining the BEF in France from May 1940. Barely a month later, he was among the troops evacuated from Dunkirk, afterwards remaining in the United Kingdom for the rest of the war. Postwar, his work as an accountant for a major national food supplier took him all over the country, to the heart of dockland in several major ports, providing an unequalled opportunity for him to get close to tugs in their working environment. This led him to specialise in the recording of steam tugs on film, concentrating on the vessels working on the rivers Thames, Tyne and Mersey and in the port of Southampton. Little did he realise how critically important his self-adopted project was to be, given that the disposal of the last craft of this type was imminent.

By the mid-1970s, the few remaining steam tugs — once the mainstay of towage in the ports of the United Kingdom — had virtually disappeared completely. Today, extremely powerful motor tugs dominate the scene, but, for all their efficient smartness, they do not exude the character of their steam predecessors as they bustled, steam-belching, around the port traffic of those days, which, equally, seemed a great deal more visually interesting than does its present-day equivalent.

Photographed in October 1975 at Stockton-on-Tees, the *John H. Amos* (202grt, 110ft) of the Tees Conservancy is another preserved steam-paddle tug, today located at Chatham as part of the Medway Maritime Museum collection. For a period after her retirement she was renamed *Hero*. A River Commissioners tug, the *John H. Amos* was constructed by Bow, McLachlan & Co at Paisley in 1931 — the last paddle tug to be built in the UK for a civilian owner. She also happened to be the last vessel delivered by her builder, for the company went bankrupt before she was even completed. Unusually for a tug of this type, her saloon was not sufficiently large to accommodate the commissioners that she was intended to carry on tours of inspection of the port installations on the River Tees.

The River Tyne, with its miles of docks and shipyards on both banks, has been described as the 'home of towage', so it is fitting that we begin our circumnavigation of the UK with the steam tugs from this region:

Above: With the new Royal Fleet Auxiliary fleet tanker *Olynthus* (A122), Tyne Tugs' *Beamish* (242grt, 113ft 6in) and, in the distance, *Joffre*. The *Beamish* was completed as the *Empire Paul* in 1944 by J. S. Watson Ltd, Gainsborough. In 1946 she was renamed *Queensgarth* for Rea Towing before a year later joining France Fenwick Tyne & Wear, where she spent a long career, based on the River Tyne.

Like many of the steam tugs which entered service during and immediately after World War 2, she was converted into a motor tug in late 1964. Ten years later, the *Beamish* was sold for continued employment at Thunder Bay, on Lake Superior, Canada, for Western Engineering Co Ltd. The *Olynthus* was renamed *Olwen* in 1967, as her original name tended to be confused with that of the *Olympus*, an 'Oberon'-class submarine. Measuring 36,000 tons full-load displacement, her overall length was 648ft. Her RFA career ended after 35 years when she was removed from the Navy List in 2000.

Right: Berthed at North Shields, three France Fenwick steam tugs: from the right, the *Cullercoats*, the *Earsdon* and, just visible, the business end of the *Wearmouth*. To the left is an unidentified Lawson-Batey tug with distinctive yellow funnel bearing a blue Maltese Cross. The *Cullercoats* (181grt, 106ft 6in) was built as the *Cyclop* in 1898 by J. P. Rennoldson, South Shields. She remained active on the River Tyne until well into the 1960s.

Below right: Moored in the River Tyne, at South Shields, the steam tugs *Earsdon* and *Beamish* in their original France Fenwick Tyne & Wear colours. Supposedly based on the uniform of the Sunderland police force, these colours were intended to convey the meaning 'Safety & Security', as per the company's motto. Built in 1912 by Bocle & Pot at Bolnes, Netherlands, the *Earsdon* (234grt, 114ft 6in) entered service under the name *Colonel Thys*. In 1932 she was renamed *Lewis Crosthwaite* before receiving her third identity in 1950.

Left: Four classic River Tyne screw steam tugs, (from left) *Francis Batey* (151 grt) built in 1914, *Waysider* (166 grt) delivered in 1919, *Tynesider* and *Joffre*, along with the motor tugs *Maximus* and *Impetus*, partly obscured, berthed at the tug anchorage, South Shields. Hall, Russell & Co of Aberdeen built the *Tynesider* (262grt, 107ft 10in) in 1942. She entered service under the name *Empire Cherub*, joining her commercial owners in 1946. All four of the steam tugs were originally members of the Lawson-Batey fleet, a company formed in 1920 by the merging of the towage interests of J. T. Batey and the Lawson Steam Tug Co.

Above: Seen here in Tyne Tugs colours, the former Lawson-Batey steam tug *Joffre* (260grt, 115ft) in a photograph taken in October 1964. Dating from 1916, the *Joffre* was constructed by the Ardrossan Shipbuilding Co. Her triple-expansion steam-reciprocating machinery gave her a power output of 1,140ihp. Built specifically for coastal towing, she was unusual for a tug of her size in having two towing hooks. The *Joffre* almost suffered a premature end in 1925 when, while on 'foreign station', she was stranded at Start Point, Devon, during a voyage from Falmouth to Antwerp. She was scrapped at Bo'ness in 1966.

General view of the South Shields tug anchorage showing numerous France Fenwick and Lawson-Batey steam tugs alongside ocean-going salvage vessels, steam tenders and naval minesweepers. In the drydock (foreground) is the Lawson-Batey tug *Homer* (157grt, 95ft 4in), built in 1915. She was involved in a valiant action only months after completion when, on 8 April 1915, she attempted to ram and sink a German submarine south of St Catherine's Point, Isle of Wight, while towing the French barque *Général de Sonis*. Somehow, both U-boat and tug managed to extricate themselves from the confrontation completely unscathed. In the distance, in the centre background of this view, can be seen one of the new Fred Olsen passenger ferries — *Blenheim* or *Braemar*. They entered the Oslo–Newcastle service in 1951 and 1952 respectively and were distinguished by their modern profile and funnels.

The former Steel & Bennie tugs *Victor* and *Campaigner* from the River Clyde are seen here in Ridley Steam Tugs ownership as the *Marty* (175grt, 106ft) and *Battleaxe* (221grt, 112ft) respectively. Both these steam tugs were built by Alexander Stephen & Sons, at Linthouse, Glasgow, the *Victor* in 1906 and the *Campaigner* in 1911. Both were provided with a greater margin of speed to give them a competitive advantage while 'seeking'; an outdated practice since World War 1, this involved searching for a tow out at sea — usually sailing ships which found it difficult to manœuvre unassisted in port approaches. In 1959, two years after joining the Ridley fleet, the *Battleaxe* was renamed again when she transferred to Lawson-Batey as the *Hillsider*. With them

are the motor tugs *Maximus* and *Impetus*, both products of the Mützelfeldtwerft GmbH shipyard at Cuxhaven, and which entered service in 1954.

In the background is the Brigham & Cowan shipyard at South Shields, which had a chequered history. Opened in 1902, it later amalgamated with the neighbouring Tyne Dock Engineering Yard and other River Tyne facilities to form North East Coast Ship Repairers Ltd. Later, after financial collapse in 1974 while under Court Line ownership, the yard was nationalised as part of British Shipbuilders. Later still, during the 1980s, it was the subject of a workers' buy-out.

Above: Three small steam tenders in the Smiths Dock, North Shields —
a photograph taken in the summer of 1965. Tender No 2 is at the rear,
No 4 can just about be made out on the front inside, while the nearest
craft is so rusty it cannot be identified. These small craft, of which there
were a total of eight, measured between 27 and 39 tons. In the drydock
in the background is an unidentified BP tanker.

Right: An unidentified steam-powered shipyard tender passes the
Tanker Finance (Shell) tanker *Asprella* at South Shields, with, beyond
her, the red and black striped funnel of a Cunard or Port Line ship.
The steam-turbine tanker *Asprella* was built in 1959 by Kieler
Howaldtswerke AG in what was then West Germany. A modest-sized oil
tanker (by later standards), she measured 12,321 tons gross, 18,250 tons
deadweight and 560ft in overall length. She was transferred to Shell
Tankers (UK) Ltd in 1981, only to be broken up at Karachi a year later.

Below: Tyne Tugs' *Wearmouth* (182grt, 95ft) revealing conspicuously the nature of her propulsive power compared with her fleetmate, the motor tug *Applesider*. The *Wearmouth* was completed in 1927 by Cochrane & Sons, Selby. The BP tanker *British Signal* is in the background. A steam turbine tanker of 23,015 tons gross (35,050 tons deadweight) and 683ft length overall, she was built in 1960 by Ansaldo SpA, Genoa.

Right: Steam paddle, steam screw and internal combustion seen together: the France Fenwick Wearside tugs *Houghton*, *Fulwell* and *Grangetown*. The paddle tug *Houghton* (133grt, 101ft) entered service in 1904. She was constructed at the Hepple & Co shipyard at North Shields. The power output of her engines at 425ihp was somewhat

lower than that of later steam tugs of comparable dimensions. Paid off in October 1964, the *Houghton* was scrapped at Dunston, near Newcastle. The *Fulwell* (149grt, 92ft 2in) was completed in 1899 as the *Nelson* for Alexandra Towing by J. Jones & Sons, Liverpool. She passed into France Fenwick ownership in 1934, remaining with the company until 1959, when she was sold for scrapping at Gateshead. The *Grangetown* was one of a pair of wartime-built motor tugs of 176 tons gross, the other being the *Ryhope*.

Fitting out at the J. Crown & Sons shipyard, in the background, is the Hall Bros motorship *Bretwalda*, which entered service in 1958. She measured 450ft length overall with a tonnage of 7,893 gross. Note too the tall funnel of an ancient steamboat in the right background, with small river tugs on either side of it.

Above: The *Souter* and the *Eppleton Hall*, two France Fenwick Tyne & Wear paddle tugs moored in the River Wear at Sunderland, with, farthest away, the diesel-engined tug *Ryhope*. By the end of the 1950s France Fenwick retained paddle tugs only on the Wear station, its last such vessel on Tyneside having been disposed of a good many years earlier. The *Eppleton Hall* (166grt, 105ft) was a large vessel, one of the last paddle tugs to be built for British owners. She was another product of the Hepple & Co yard at North Shields, having been completed for Lambton & Hetton Collieries, for which she worked for 30 years. She joined France Fenwick in 1945 for service at Sunderland. In keeping with North East coast practice, the *Eppleton Hall* had a tow-hook mounted on a Samson post in the bow. She is one of the few paddle-driven tugs to have survived the passing of the steam era. Sold to Seaham Harbour Co in 1964, she became surplus to requirements three years later and was sold for demolition. However, she was subsequently reprieved, and, after a thorough overhaul, she crossed the Atlantic under her own steam and then passed through the Panama Canal to reach San Francisco, for preservation there as a working museum exhibit.

Right: Another view of the *Eppleton Hall*, with the *Souter* and, behind them, the *Houghton*, the *Fulwell* and the *Grangetown*. Built in 1910 by J. P. Rennoldson & Sons at South Shields, the *Souter* (123grt, 91ft) first entered service with the Sunderland Towage Co. She was scrapped at Blyth from January 1964.

Another paddle tug belonging to France Fenwick, the *Roker* (119grt, 100ft) was built by J. P. Rennoldson & Sons in 1904. Many years later, after transfer to the Grangemouth & Forth Towing Co, the *Roker* became the last paddle tug to be stationed at Methil, Fife, on Scotland's east coast, from 1962 to 1966; her service was short-lived, however, for she was already in a seriously run-down condition and fit only for scrap.

In the background of this view taken on the River Wear is (on the right) the Constantine Shipping Co's motor cargo ship *Thameswood*. Registered at Middlesbrough, she was built in 1957 by the Ailsa Shipbuilding Co, at Troon, and measured 1,797 tons gross and 271ft in length. To the left is the 250ft, 1,588grt *John Charrington*, owned by the Charrington Steamship Co and built locally by J. Crown & Sons, Sunderland. Note the three boys playing on the tug's forward paddle wheel sponson.

Above: Photographed together at Seaham Harbour are the paddle tugs *Seaham* and *Reliant*, both belonging to the Seaham Harbour Dock Co. The *Reliant* (156grt, 100ft) was built in 1907 by J. T. Eltringham & Co, South Shields, as the *Old Trafford* for the Manchester Shipping Canal Co. Her engines were of the side-lever or 'grasshopper' configuration. Another distinctive feature of her design was that her paddle sponsons extended either side of the paddle wheels out as far as her bow and her stern. The *Reliant* received her new name in 1951 after she was bought by Ridley Steam Tugs. Her working career ended in 1969, but she survives today as an exhibit at the National Maritime Museum, built into the Neptune Hall displays at Romney Road, Greenwich.

Right: The *Seaham* (133grt, 90ft 4in) again — a closer view of her, taken on 8 April 1958. Completed in 1909 by J. P. Rennoldson, South Shields, she survived until October 1962, when she was sold for breaking-up by J. J. King & Co on Tyneside. *R. C. Riley*

Formed in 1921 by a group of Hull towing concerns, the United Towing Co's name remains synonymous with ocean towing and salvage — a business traditionally dominated by Dutch firms. This is the company's *Guardsman* (329grt, 123ft 6in), a vessel built in 1946 as the *Empire Nina* by Cochrane & Sons, Selby; United Towing acquired her in 1947. During World War 2, Government concern that the Admiralty and the Ministry of War Transport had insufficient tugs available to them prompted it to launch a programme of new construction based on three prototypes, each of which was considered to be the best of its type. For river work, ship-handling purposes in port and short coastal voyages, Steel & Bennie's *Warrior*, built in 1935, was selected as the model. A large number of tugs of this type were therefore built, all with names beginning with 'Empire' and known variously as the 'Warrior' and 'Modified Warrior' class. The *Guardsman* was one of this type, as were the *Rifleman*, *Napia*, *Cervia*, *Beamish* and other tugs shown elsewhere in this book. She is seen here berthed at Thameshaven in July 1963.

Above: A slightly smaller tug from the United Towing fleet, the 1938-built *Krooman* (230grt, 106ft), another product of Cochrane & Sons, Selby, replaced an earlier vessel of the same name. Unlike some of the bigger United Towing Co vessels, the *Krooman* was used primarily for docks and river work in the Humber. She is seen leaving the Royal Terrace Pier, Gravesend, with an Elliott steam tug ahead of her.

Right: Similar to the *Guardsman*, the *Rifleman* (ex-*Empire Vera*) (333grt, 123ft 6in) was also built by Cochrane & Sons at Selby, in 1945, passing to the United Towing fleet in 1947; this view dates from August 1966. Since that time, United Towing has converted entirely to diesel-powered craft, and the company now owns some of the most powerful ocean tugs afloat.

Left: The *Atlantic Cock* (182grt, 96ft), seen here near the Royal Terrace Pier, Gravesend in her original Gamecock Tugs colours. Built in 1932 by A. Hall & Co at Aberdeen, the *Atlantic Cock* was one of a group of three vessels of the same size, the others being the *Crested Cock* and the *Ocean Cock*. During World War 2 the *Atlantic Cock* was severely damaged by a mine which exploded under the nearby *Flying Kite* of the Clyde Shipping Co; the Clyde vessel sank, damaged beyond repair. The *Atlantic Cock* was broken up at Antwerp from February 1970. Beyond her in this picture is one of the Swedish-flag freighters of the Dan-Axel Brostrom Co.

Above: The river tug *Blue Circle* (111grt, 83ft) was owned by Associated Portland Cement Manufacturers Ltd, a company which had some nine tugs operating on the Thames, employed in lighter towage. In all, the company owned more than 20 tugs. The *Blue Circle* was built in 1927 at Lytham, Lancashire, by the Lytham Shipbuilding & Engineering Co.

Left: William Watkins Ltd was the first true commercial tug owner, being established on the River Thames in 1833. Over the ensuing years the company came to dominate the towage business in the Port of London and along the Thames, and by the mid-1950s a fleet of 11 large tugs was being operated, all steam-powered. Gradually, new tugs of comparable size and fitted with internal combustion engines were introduced, replacing the steam tugs. The *Cervia* (233grt, 113ft), one of Watkins' last steam tugs, was acquired in 1947, having been completed a year earlier by A. Hall & Co, Aberdeen, as the *Empire Raymond*. She

is shown here in Ship Towage colours in April 1969. The *Cervia* has since been preserved at Ramsgate by the East Kent Maritime Museum.

Above: An earlier view of the *Cervia*, at Tilbury Docks in March 1963, assisting the P&O passenger mail liner *Iberia*. The second of two new ships built for the Australian services in the mid-1950s, the 29,614grt *Iberia* made her maiden voyage on the London–Sydney route on 28 September 1954. While assisting the *Iberia's* sister-ship *Arcadia*, in 1954, the *Cervia* capsized and sank at Tilbury.

Left: The *Contest* (213grt, 108ft), another A. Hall & Co-built vessel, was the last steam tug to join the Elliott fleet, entering service in 1933. Like the *Challenge*, she exhibited particular features associated with this builder, notably her distinctive elliptical stern. She carries Ship Towage colours, in part based on her previous Elliott livery, in which the funnel was all black apart from the chequered red/white house flag. The *Contest*'s career ended in 1972, when she was paid off for disposal and scrapped at Grays. This photograph of her was taken five years earlier, in January 1967.

Below: The former Elliott steam tugs *Challenge* and *Contest* moored in the river with William Watkins' motor tug *Ionia* in February 1967. The *Challenge* (212grt, 100ft) was completed in 1931 by A. Hall & Co, Aberdeen. Today, she lies in St Katherine's Dock, London, as a preserved example of the Port of London's once huge fleet of steam tugs.

Right: On the slipway at Denton, East Sussex, the *Danube V* (241grt, 110ft 6in), owned by the Tilbury Contracting & Dredging Co, in a picture that shows off well the typical underwater form of a tug. She seems to have a plain black-painted funnel, which is not in accordance with her owner's original or later colours. Cochrane & Sons of Selby completed her in 1935 along with the virtually identical *Danube VI*.

Above: The *Danube VI* in the original Tilbury Contracting & Dredging Co colours, moving a hopper barge (visible in the background). The tugs of the Tilbury Contracting & Dredging Co were engaged primarily in moving dredgers around the river and in towing barges of silt and mud for dumping or unloading at land-fill sites, but they were also used occasionally for ship-handling.

Right: The *Danube VII* (237grt, 118ft 6in) was a postwar addition to the Tilbury Contracting & Dredging Co fleet, commissioned in 1946. Like most tug operators, the company tended to use one builder for new construction, and indeed the *Danube VII*, like many of her predecessors, was constructed by Cochrane & Sons, Selby. In this photograph, taken in September 1966, her colours have been changed, reflecting the restyling (from the early 1960s) of her owner as the London Dredging Co. In the background, to the right, is a group of moored Sun tugs.

Above: Ship-towage tug *Gondia* (200grt, 107ft) in Gravesend Reach, with the Tilbury Power Station on the far shore. Another tug built by Cochrane & Sons, she entered service in 1927. From the outbreak of World War 2 the *Gondia*, along with her fleetmate *Simla* and Gamecock Tugs' *Watercock*, was moved to Dover to perform harbour duties there as well as to be available to assist ships in Channel convoys that were in distress. They performed valiantly when the port activity intensified enormously during the Dunkirk evacuation, the harbour having become clogged with traffic. In no small way, by keeping everything moving, they helped to ensure the operation was a success. The *Gondia* was scrapped in 1966.

Right: A superb view of the William Watkins steam tug *Java* (128grt, 100ft), completed by Cochrane & Sons, Selby, in 1905. She is seen here in Limehouse Reach outside the Greenland Dock — part of the Surrey Commercial Docks group and one of the oldest in the London Docks complex, dating from the late 17th century. During the Dunkirk evacuation, the *Java* rendered heroic assistance to the Clyde paddle steamer *Waverley* after the latter was bombed and sunk by German aircraft on 29 May 1940. The *Java* rescued 120 of the *Waverley*'s complement of troops, landing them at Ramsgate the next day. She was scrapped at Benfleet, Essex, in 1965.

The *Napia* (261grt, 114ft), here in Ship Towage colours, was built by the Goole Shipbuilding & Repair Co, entering Admiralty service in 1943 as the *Empire Jester*; William Watkins took her over in 1946. She remained in employment on the Thames through a sequence of reorganisations of the tug fleets on the river, until London Tugs sold her

in December 1971 to Greek owners who based her at Piraeus under the new name *Tolmiros*. She continued to operate for a further 14 years until disposed of for scrap in February 1986 and broken up at Perama. More than 40 years after she was built, she was still running her original steam reciprocating engines.

Another view of the *Napia*, here towing British India's *Nuddea* through one of the entrance locks to the King George V Dock in the Port of London's Royal Docks group. The 8,513grt *Nuddea* was a single-screw steamship, constructed at Glasgow by Barclay, Curle & Co and entering service in August 1954. She was the lead ship of a class of four high-speed cargo liners for the UK–Australia trade (her sisters being the *Nowshera*, *Nardana* and *Nyanza*) which were built to a completely new postwar design with capacity for 28,000cu ft of refrigerated cargo. Accommodation was also provided for two passengers. With the imminent containerisation of the UK–Australia cargo service, the

Nuddea was switched to the Japan–Persian Gulf run in 1967. Meanwhile, two of here sisters — the *Nyanza* and the *Nardana* — had been transferred to P&O in November 1964 as the *Balranald* and the *Baradine* respectively. The *Nuddea* herself passed to P&O ownership in April 1972 as part of the general reorganisation of group cargo services. However, she became an early casualty of the oil crisis of the 1970s: the high fuel consumption of her boilers made her uneconomic to operate, and she was sold in February 1973 for dismantling in Kaohsiung, Taiwan.

Left: The *Ocean Cock* (182grt, 96ft), painted in her original Gamecock Tugs colours, photographed in the Tilbury drydock. Built by A. Hall & Co, Aberdeen, she was completed in 1932. Along with her fleetmates she was absorbed into the Ship Towage group formed in 1950, and subsequently adopted the colours of the consortium.

Right: A later view of the former Gamecock Tugs *Ocean Cock* in October 1967, now painted in the colours of Gaselee & Son Ltd, for operation at Felixstowe. Gaselee's larger tugs were by this time linked with the Ship Towage consortium. The *Ocean Cock* survived until 1969 when she was sold for breaking-up in Belgium.

The Port of London Authority tug *Lea* (54grt, 71ft) was built as TID168, one of a large group of small steam tugs completed during wartime for the Admiralty; she was completed in 1946 by R. Dunston Ltd at Hessle on the River Humber. Designed for rapid construction for lighterage and dock work, the TID class had straight (rather than curved) plates in the hull. Some were retained for naval dockyard use after the end of the war, but most were snapped up by commercial towage concerns. This photograph of the *Lea* was taken in October 1967.

William Watkins' *Racia* (163grt, 100ft) in the King George V Dock. Completed in 1930 as the *Dilwara* by Cochrane & Sons, Selby, five years later she was renamed *Dendera* and three years after that was purchased for the Watkins fleet. The *Racia* was another tug which excelled at the time of the evacuation of the BEF from Dunkirk, rescuing 373 troops on two crossings to the beaches — the greatest total rescued by any single Thames tug involved in the operation.

With the *Racia* in this photograph can be seen the Shaw Savill & Albion motor liner *Dominion Monarch* and, to the left, the stern of the Glen Line's *Radnorshire*. Built by Swan Hunter & Wigham Richardson at Wallsend-on-Tyne, the *Dominion Monarch* was the largest passenger liner ever owned and operated by Shaw Savill Line, at 27,155 tons gross and 682ft length overall. She made her maiden voyage from Southampton to Wellington, New Zealand, on 17 February 1939, but, after only a few round voyages, her service was interrupted by the outbreak of war. Following gruelling wartime service, which included a narrow escape from Singapore just before it fell to the Japanese, she resumed her commercial career at the end of 1948. Fourteen years later she was sold for scrapping in Osaka, Japan. The 7,632grt *Radnorshire* was completed for Blue Funnel in 1948 as the *Achilles*, having been constructed by the Caledon Shipbuilding & Engineering Co at Dundee. She transferred to Glen Line after just one year under the Alfred Holt & Co house flag.

Above: Built back in 1898 by Lobnitz & Co, Renfrew, the *Simla* (144grt, 104ft) was originally rigged to carry gaff sails on two masts, with a staysail forward. She was a typical 'seeking' tug of her time, with a slender hull for greater speed and a good standard of accommodation for her crew, who were obliged to spend long periods on board. Her sister tug, the *Harold*, was built for S. Pearson & Sons, London. She was requisitioned for war service from 1914 to 1915, during which time her crew salvaged the *Sarpen*, which had stranded in the Orkney Islands; otherwise she spent her entire career with William Watkins, until disposed of in 1964. She is seen here in London's Royal Docks with Houlder Bros' 10,785grt refrigerated motorship *Hornby Grange*, built in 1946 by Hawthorn, Leslie & Co at Hebburn-on-Tyne. Engaged in the South American meat trade, the *Hornby Grange* passed to Royal

Mail as the *Douro* in February 1969 before transferring again to Prince Line. She was broken up at Aviles, Spain, from June 1972.

Right: The *Sun IV* (200grt, 116ft 6in), owned by W. H. J. Alexander — better known as Sun Tugs — towing the Liberian-registered *Seaspray* into the King George V Dock. The *Sun IV*, along with her sister tug *Sun V*, was built in 1915 by Earles Shipbuilding Co, Hull. The 7,111grt Liberty Ship (No 2114) *Seaspray* (ex-*Citta di Viareggio*), owned by Seaspray Shipping Co, Monrovia, since 1962, started life as the *Peter Cooper Hewitt*, built by the Permanente Shipyard No 1 at Richmond, Virginia, in 1943. She was scrapped at Venice from February 1967. The *Sun IV* was sold in 1966, becoming the *San Benigo*.

Left: Towing the Greek motorship *Ocean Seigneur* (ex-*Capetan Yemelos*) from the King George V Dock, the *Sun XI* (183grt, 106ft 6in) was one of a group of similar tugs (the others being the *Sun XII* to *Sun XV*) all built by Earles Shipbuilding Co, Hull. Completed in 1925, they were the last large tugs to join the Sun Tugs fleet before World War 2. Owned by Cia Ultramarine SA since 1959, the *Ocean Seigneur* was built by Hitachi Zosen in 1956. After numerous renamings — *Yinka Folawayo* in 1975, *Maldive Prize* in 1980, *Dynasty Utheem* in 1984 and *Island Queen*, also in 1984 — she was scrapped in 1986. On the far side of the dock is one of Royal Mail Line's 'Highland'-class motor passenger ships, originally built for Nelson Line by Harland & Wolff, Belfast, between 1928 and 1932, for employment on the London–La Plata ports service. The *Sun XI* was sold to Scheldt Towage,

Antwerp, in late 1964, becoming the *Scheldex*. She was later resold to Italian owners and renamed *Andrea*.

Above: Sister tug to the *Sun XI*, the *Sun XII* is seen here with the Shahristan Steamship Co (Frank C. Strick) steamship *Muristan*, in a photograph taken in October 1963. Built by J. Readhead & Sons, South Shields, the 8,408grt *Muristan* entered service in 1950 on the London–Persian Gulf route. In 1966 she was sold to Greek owners as the *Leonis*, and two years later became the *Atlas Trader* under the South Korean flag. Her next move, in 1970, took her to Liberian ownership as the *Yaling*, her career ending two years later when she was broken up at Kaohsiung, Taiwan. The *Sun XII*, meanwhile, was broken up in Belgium in 1969.

After World War 2, Sun Tugs took delivery of two larger steam tugs, completed, unlike their predecessors, by A. Hall & Co, Aberdeen. These were the *Sun XVI* (ex-*Empire Leonard*) and *Sun XVII* (both 233grt, 113ft), which entered service in 1946. The picture shows the *Sun XVI* with other tugs in Gravesend Reach, off the Royal Terrace Pier. Behind

her, in mid-river, is the 469grt coastal tanker *Tempo* (ex-*Pan* 1956, ex-*Pando* 1946, ex-*Chant 62* 1946) being assisted by a small Port of London Authority tug. The *Tempo* was owned by Rederi A/B, Björnö, Sweden, and had been built in 1944 by the Furness Shipbuilding Co at Haverton Hill. The *Sun XVI* was sold in 1962 and renamed *San Cataldo*.

Below: The *Sun XVII* — a photograph taken in April 1966.
The Sun Tug Co (W. H. J. Alexander) was established in 1883.

Right: Another view of the *Sun XVII*, here seen with the
Angfartygs A/B Tirfing (Dan-Axel Brostrom)-owned *Kronoland*,
registered at Gothenburg. This 5,083grt motorship, built in 1951
by Eriksburg Mekanika Verksted A/B, was strengthened for ice
navigation. The photograph dates from September 1964.

Above: Gamecock Tugs' 1923-built *Watercock* (ex-*Masterman*) (200grt, 96ft 7in), escorting a Shaw Savill & Albion ship in August 1967. The latter appears to be the *Waipawa* — the only surviving vessel of six prewar 'W'-class 'Empire Food Ships'. These large refrigerated motorships, all built by Harland & Wolff at either Belfast or Glasgow, had 500,000cu ft of capacity for refrigerated cargo and accommodation for 12 passengers. This is one of the last pictures of the *Waipawa*, taken during her final season with the Shaw Savill Line. She was sold for scrapping in Taiwan the following year.

Right: Another wonderful view of a Thames steam tug, the Port of London Authority's *Westbourne* (185grt, 102ft) photographed in August 1964, towards the end of her working career. She had been built by Cammell Laird & Co at Birkenhead in 1912.

Three Admiralty tugs at Chatham, (from the left) the *Diver* (102grt, 89ft), the *Prompt* (232grt, 113ft) and the *Energetic* (234grt), the latter pair being designated Fleet Servicing Tugs. By the time this picture was taken, responsibility for ship-handling craft at Royal Navy bases had passed from the Directorate of Dockyards to the Port Auxiliary Service.

The diesel-engined *Diver*, along with a sister tug, the *Dipper*, was a war-prize, both being former German mine-location vessels, built in Hamburg in 1943 as Nos C28 and C30 respectively. After several moves, including spells of duty at Port Edgar, Chatham and Rosyth and, from 1963, at Singapore, the *Diver* was acquired by the Singapore Government in April 1971.

The *Prompt* began life as the *Empire Spitfire*, completed in 1943 by A. Hall & Co. Four years later, while stationed at Malta, she was renamed *Warden*, becoming the *Prompt* in 1951. In 1957 she was moved

to Chatham, remaining there until she was sold to Thames Towage Services, Tilbury, in July 1975, at which time she was renamed yet again, becoming the *Torque*. She is now preserved at the Maryport Maritime Museum, Cumbria.

Another wartime newbuilding and one of the oil-fired vessels of her class, the *Energetic* entered service in 1942. Completed as the *Empire Ned*, she was renamed *Empire Edward* in March 1945. Until October 1954 she was engaged in naval service at Trieste under the auspices of the Allied Military Government. After being moved briefly to Malta, she was transferred to the UK — allocated to Chatham Dockyard — in May 1955, when she was renamed *Energetic*. In 1965 she was sold to Greek owner Tsavliris as the *Nisos Lefkos*. Ten years later she was renamed again — as the *Kronos* — following purchase by another Piraeus-based salvage and towage concern.

Moored in the Medway at Chatham on 6 August 1978 as the *Goliath*, the former Admiralty steam tug *Eminent* (295grt, 124ft) was completed in 1946 as the *Empire Tessa* and first renamed in August 1947. Initially allocated to Bermuda, she suffered serious fire damage there in January 1951 and was returned to the UK. She remained in Portsmouth Dockyard until February 1969, at which time she transferred to the Clyde. In August 1975 the Medway Maritime Museum took her into its ownership and she was towed south by the one-time Watkins Thames tug *Cervia*, which can be seen lying alongside her in this picture. Renaming as the *Goliath* evidently occurred some time between late 1975 and the time of this picture. The significance of the letters 'ITL' on the funnels of both tugs is not known. The *Goliath* was subsequently moved to the Maryport Maritime Museum collection in Cumbria.

Left: Photographed at Chatham in June 1974, the oil-fired Fleet Servicing Tug *Resolve* (ex-*Empire Zona*) (290grt, 124ft), built in 1946, moored in mid-stream alongside the Greek-flagged *Atlas*, both vessels being viewed over the stern of dockyard tug TID164.

Based initially on the River Clyde, the *Empire Zona* was attached to the Directorate of Boom Defence and was manned by RFA personnel. Later, in December 1957, she was transferred to the Port Auxiliary Service at Chatham, where she was renamed *Resolve* in June 1958. For just over a year from November 1969 she performed trials at Rosyth as a Basin Tug, but she then returned to Chatham, where she was put up for sale in October 1973, duly passing to Greek owners for continued operation.

Over 180 of the utility TID-class tugs were built from 1943 to 1945. All their main sections were prefabricated by 'dispersed' engineering contractors, to reduce the risk of interruption to production by enemy bombing, and were shipped by road to temporary slipways for assembly and launching. From November 1945, when she was completed, TID164 was attached to HMS Lochinvar at Port Edgar, where she performed general harbour duties. After five years in reserve at Rosyth she was reactivated in 1962 and remained in use until June 1974, when

she was sold to the Medway Maritime Museum for preservation in Chatham Historic Dockyard.

Above: Since the mid-1800s, at least one tug has been regularly stationed at Dover to provide a convenient salvage capability for ships coming to grief on the nearby Goodwin Sands. This is the Dover Harbour Board's large and powerful twin-funnel, twin-screw tug *Lady Brassey* (362grt, 130ft), built in 1913 by J. P. Rennoldson at South Shields. In addition to her salvage function, she doubled as a tender tug. Her full-width wheelhouse was unusual. During World War 1 she more than once risked minefields to go to the aid of vessels in distress, but 25 years later she earned greater acclaim during Operation 'Dynamo', the Dunkirk Evacuation, when, in consort with the *Foremost 87*, she helped to re-float the LNER short-sea ferry *Prague*, which had gone aground at Dunkirk. After assisting the *Prague* out of Dunkirk harbour, the *Lady Brassey* proceeded to tow her to Deal, where she arrived on 1 June 1940. Two days later, another ferry, the Southern Railway's *Paris*, was not so lucky. Despite the efforts of the Thames tug *Sun XV* to tow her to safety, she sank in mid-Channel. The *Lady Brassey* was scrapped in 1958, overtaken by powerful diesel-engined ocean tugs.

Left: Three Alexandra Towing Co steam tugs in Southampton's Ocean Dock: the *Brambles* (242grt, 113ft 6in), the *Flying Kestrel* (244grt, 114ft) and the *Formby* (237grt, 109ft). Beyond them, at Berth 46, is the Cunard passenger liner *Mauretania*, painted green for cruise operations. The photograph was taken in April 1964. The *Brambles* and the *Flying Kestrel* were both members of the Admiralty's 'Warrior' class. The *Brambles* was built by Henry Scarr at Hessle on Humberside as the *Empire Teak*, entering service in 1942. The *Flying Kestrel* was built at the same shipyard in 1943 as the *Empire Mascot*; four years later she was renamed *Metinda IV* for Metal Industries Ltd. Alexandra Towing acquired the pair in 1950 and 1951 respectively.

Cunard's 35,655grt, 772ft-long *Mauretania*, the second ship of the name, was built by Cammell Laird & Co and made her maiden voyage to New York in June 1939. Never intended to be a 'racer' like her predecessor, she worked the intermediate transatlantic service to New York from London, Liverpool or Southampton. After distinguished wartime auxiliary service and a peacetime career which suffered to some extent for want of a consistent role, she was broken up at Inverkeithing from 1965.

The *Flying Kestrel* and the *Brambles* were broken up in 1969 and 1971 respectively, the former at Passage West, Cork, the latter at Newport, Monmouthshire. The *Formby* escaped the cutter's torch. Renamed *Poderoso*, she was sold in 1969 for continued operation with Fratelli Baretta Fu Domenico, Brindisi.

Above: Built in 1923 by John I. Thornycroft, with a sister, *Clausentum*, the *Canute* (271grt, 111ft) served Red Funnel at Southampton for 42 years. Like all Red Funnel tugs, she was twin-screw. During World War 2 she was sunk at Southampton by a German bomb on 28 December 1940. She was raised and repaired, continuing with towage duties in the port for another 25 years, finally being sold to Greek owners in 1965 and renamed *Nisos Samos*. In the background in this view is another of Alexandra Towing Co's steam tugs, the *Canada* (237grt, 100ft 8in), completed in 1951. In 1969, along with her sister the *Formby*, the *Canada* was sold to Brindisi tug owners, becoming the *Strepitoso*.

Beyond the tugs is one of the two Channel Island ferries — *Caesarea* and *Sarnia* — belonging to British Railways' Southern Region. These 4,174grt vessels, with accommodation for 1,400 passengers, were built by J. Samuel White & Co at Cowes, Isle of Wight, both entering service in the spring of 1961.

Below: At the time she joined Red Funnel (Southampton, Isle of Wight & South of England Royal Mail Steam Packet), the twin-screw tender tug *Calshot* (684grt, 147ft), built in 1930 by John I. Thornycroft at Woolston, Southampton, was the most powerful tug in its fleet, with a power output of 1,500ihp. She is seen alongside one of Union Castle Line's lavender-hulled Cape mail liners that were celebrated for their 'Every Thursday at four o'clock' departures until July 1965, when an accelerated mail service was implemented. Following conversion to diesel propulsion, increasing her power output to 1,800bhp, the *Calshot* was sold in 1964 to Port & Liner Services (Ireland) Ltd. Renamed *Galway Bay*, she was used as a ferry on Ireland's west coast, carrying as many as 400 passengers.

Left: The *Calshot* again, this time seen from the deck of the Greek Line's passenger ship *Arkadia;* after some 24 years in Ireland, the *Calshot* returned to Southampton and is now preserved in the port under her original name, owned by Southampton Maritime Museum and located at Berth 41 in the Eastern Docks.

Another tender tug based at Southampton, Alexandra Towing Co's *Flying Breeze* (second of the name) in the Ocean Dock with, beyond her, the steam tug *Canada*, on the inside, and the new diesel tug *Ventnor*. The *Flying Breeze* (460grt, 128ft 6in) was built as the *Zurmand* in 1938 by Scott & Sons, Bowling, to work in the Middle East oil ports. In 1955 she was renamed *BP Protector*, passing to Alexandra Towing in 1961 for which she was converted on the Clyde for tendering work. She was

the last true steam-powered tender to operate in the United Kingdom.

To the right of the three tugs can be seen the landward end of the Ocean Terminal building. Opened on 31 July 1950 by Prime Minister Clement Attlee, this was the United Kingdom's principal embarkation point for the Atlantic ferry. It was demolished in the early 1980s, but a replica has since been constructed at Port Canaveral, Florida, for the new Disney Corporation cruise ships.

Above: Another view of the *Flying Breeze*, revealing some of the typical design features of a tender tug: the built-up superstructure comprising an additional full-length promenade deck and, in her case, partially-enclosed main deck housing the passenger accommodation. In 1968 Alexandra Towing sold her to Tsavliris, Piraeus, which renamed her *Nisos Thira*.

Right: Working alongside each other in June 1963, assisting the giant Cunard liner *Queen Mary*, are Alexandra Towing's *Flying Kestrel* and Red Funnel's *Sir Bevois* (318grt, 123ft). Out of sight, to the right, is a third tug, the *Thorness*, a Red Funnel diesel craft. The previous *Sir Bevois* was a wartime bombing casualty, sunk at Plymouth on 20 March 1941; the tug shown here, named in commemoration of the war loss, was introduced in 1953, built locally by John I. Thornycroft. Red Funnel sold her in 1968 as more diesel-powered tugs joined its fleet. The tugs based at Southampton, like those shown here, were characteristically powerful, to enable them to handle the large passenger liners using the port; the *Sir Bevois*'s engines developed 1,500ihp. In the distance, berthed at the New or Western Docks, can be seen one of Union Castle's Cape mail liners.

Alexandra Towing Co's *Gladstone* (237grt, 109ft), seen berthed in Southampton's Old Docks, was built in 1951 by Cochrane & Sons at

Selby. Sold in 1968 to Italian owner Societa Anonima Italiana Lavori Edili Maritimi, based at Palermo, she was renamed *Archimede S*.

Right: Steaming up Southampton Water, bound from the Fawley Oil Refinery to the Docks, is Red Funnel's *Hamtun* (318grt, 129ft), completed in 1953 and sister tug to the second *Sir Bevois*. The pair were Red Funnel's last steam tugs and the only ones to have oil-fired boilers. Like her sister, the *Hamtun* was built at Woolston on the River Itchen by John I. Thornycroft. This photograph of her was taken in May 1965; five years later she was converted to diesel propulsion and sold on for continued operation in the port of Antwerp, re-entering service as the *Natalie Letzer*. Red Funnel's involvement in ship towage at Southampton began in 1887 when the company took over the New Southampton Steam Towing Co and its existing fleet of four tugs.

Below right: Berthed in Southampton's Empress Dock are Red Funnel's tender tug *Paladin* and the conventional ship-handling tugs *Neptune* and *Canute*.

The *Paladin* (332grt, 140ft) was completed in 1913 for Anchor Line, serving its passenger ships operating from the Clyde; Red Funnel acquired her from the Clyde Shipping Co in 1946. She had a slender beam for a tender tug, necessitating the placement of her boilers in tandem and resulting in her having sufficient space only for a first-class saloon; other passengers were obliged to sit or stand on her open decks, with just her promenade deck cover as protection from the elements. Briefly renamed *Paladin II*, she was sold for scrap at Rotterdam in 1960.

The *Neptune* (314grt, 130ft) was an even older tug, built in 1910 by Day, Summers & Co at Northam, Southampton, along with the similar tugs *Hector* and *Sir Bevois* (first of the name). All three were very powerful, twin-screw tugs, coal-fired throughout their lives, with compound steam engines producing between 1,400 and 1,600ihp. As comparatively large conventional tugs, they could be used to carry passengers when circumstances dictated. The *Neptune*'s career with Red Funnel ended in 1961. Astern of the three tugs is the steam-reciprocating oil-sludge ship *Tulipfield* (ex-*Nordland*). Owned by British Wheeler Process Ltd of Liverpool, this 390grt vessel was built by Reiherstieg Schiffswerke in 1922, passing into British ownership in 1948.

Left: The Admiralty steam paddle tug *Camel* (412grt, 152ft 6in) was a member of the 'Robust' class, a group of 10 tugs with a bollard pull of 10 tons completed for dockyard duties between 1907 and 1915.
The *Camel* (Pennant No W38) was launched by Bow, McLachlan & Co at Paisley on 19 October 1914 and was accepted into Admiralty service, based at Devonport, the following year. Tugs of this type had their engines at main-deck level, so that the cranks and pistons were clearly visible through the square windows along their sides. The engines produced 1,250ihp, driving independent paddle wheels fitted with feathering blades. The *Camel* was present at the Coronation Fleet Review at Spithead in June 1953. Just under a decade later, in 1962, when almost 50 years of age, she was sold to Haulbowline Industries, County Cork. She is seen here the previous year, on 26 August 1961, at Devonport Dockyard, with, alongside her, the 1946-built twin-screw

steam tug *Careful* (1,215 tons full-load displacement). The latter's power output of 3,000ihp was almost treble that of the *Camel*.
R. C. Riley

Above: Besides its operations at Southampton and Liverpool, Alexandra Towing also maintained a fleet of tugs at Swansea. This is the *Waterloo* (200grt, 102ft), photographed at Swansea in March 1969. While some of the company's tugs spent their entire careers on a single station, others moved regularly between ports, and it was therefore not unusual for certain tugs to be seen at more than one location. The *Waterloo* was built in 1954 by Cochrane & Sons, Selby. After 18 years' operation, principally at Liverpool, she sailed from that port on 14 February 1972 bound for Italy. Purchased by the Societa Rimorchiato Napoletani, she was renamed *Dritto*.

Above: The Rea Towing Co tugs *Aysgarth* (231grt, 103ft) — nearer the camera — and *Willowgarth* (230grt) at the Princes Landing Stage, Liverpool, in July 1967. The *Aysgarth* was built in 1950 by A. Hall & Co, Aberdeen. The *Willowgarth*, a motor tug, was completed nine years later at the P. K. Harris (Shipbuilders) Ltd yard at Appledore, Devon. Rea Towing was part of the William Cory Group, which operated tugs under this name on the River Thames.

Right: Sister tug to the *Aysgarth*, this is the steam tug *Bangarth* (231grt, 103ft), completed a year later by the same builder. In October 1969 the *Bangarth* was sold to the Antwerp company SA Remorque a Helice but was subsequently lost in tow. Like the Alexandra Towing Co, Rea operated tug fleets or single vessels at several British ports — besides at Liverpool, also at Avonmouth, Cardiff, Barry and Southampton.

Below: This rather murky picture — caused partly by the smoke belching from coal-fired steam boilers — shows the Johnston Warren Line sister tugs *Ceemore* and *Deemore* (both 187grt, 104ft) in Liverpool's Gladstone Dock. Judging by the colours on its funnel, the vessel they are towing is a Houlder Line cargo ship. The *Ceemore* and *Deemore* were both built locally, by Cammell Laird & Co at Birkenhead, entering service, along with a third vessel, the *Beemore*, in 1929/30. Johnston Warren Line was one of a small number of deep-sea shipping lines that also operated port tugs, others being Anchor, Cunard and White Star. The tugs depicted here later joined Alexandra Towing: the *Ceemore* became the *Murton* in 1959, continuing until 1964 when she was scrapped at Briton Ferry; the *Deemore*, renamed *Margam* in 1958, ended her career likewise in 1965 at Silloth on the Solway Firth. The *Beemore* was also transferred to Alexandra Towing, as the *Mumbles*, and was broken up in 1965 on the River Neath.

Right: Built in 1909, the Liverpool Screw Towing & Lighterage Co's *East Cock* (139grt, 95ft), with distinctive yellow funnel and black Admiralty cowl, is seen here in one of the locks in the Gladstone Dock complex. The *East Cock* typifies the steam-powered ship-handling tugs of the River Mersey. She was single-screwed and, like most of the tugs built for towage work in this region, she had no capstan in the afterdeck and only a single towing-bow or arch. Built by Cammell Laird & Co, Birkenhead, she had a long career, serving the same owner throughout, until broken up in 1960 at Bromborough on the Mersey. Note the metal cock emblem at the top of her mast, a feature of the Liverpool 'Cock' tugs.

Left: The original tender tug *Flying Breeze* (387grt, 134ft), berthed in the Gladstone Dock with fleetmate *Crosby* (215grt, 103ft). Built for Alexandra Towing Co by J. T. Eltringham & Co, South Shields, the *Flying Breeze* entered service at Liverpool in 1913. She was small by comparison with other Liverpool tenders of her time, the two largest and longest being Cunard's *Skirmisher* (612grt, 165ft) built in 1884 and White Star Line's *Magnetic* (619grt, 170ft 6in) completed seven years later. The more recent *Crosby* was built in 1937 by Cochrane & Sons at Selby. Prior to her disposal in 1961, following the introduction of her newer namesake at Southampton, the *Flying Breeze* was briefly renamed *Flying Breeze II*. She was broken up in 1962 at Passage West, Cork. Note the unusual style of lettering used for her name, painted on the bow.

Right: A postwar addition to the Alexandra Towing Co's fleet, the *Formby* began her working career in 1951, replacing an earlier tug of the same name and spending time at both Southampton and Liverpool. Like so many other steam tugs, she was built at Selby by Cochrane & Sons. Unlike the unidentified Alexandra Towing tug to her right, she has an enclosed flying bridge.

   Behind the roof of the quayside warehouses can be seen the funnel of one of Cunard Line's four-ship 22,000grt 'Saxonia' class of Canadian-service mail liners. This would be either the *Sylvania* or the *Carinthia*, as the other pair, the *Saxonia* and the *Ivernia*, were based at Southampton.

Left: A sub-division of Liverpool Screw Towing & Lighterage was North West Tugs Ltd, formed in 1951 and the owner of *Game Cock V* (218grt, 105ft 6in) shown here. Her colours were identical to those of the other 'Cock' tugs on the Mersey, all of which had cowl-topped funnels. Cammell Laird & Co at Birkenhead was the builder of the *Game Cock V*, delivering her to her owner in 1953. Here, she is preparing to assist the Japanese-flagged cargo ship behind her, as it leaves its berth. On 9 September 1970 the *Game Cock V* passed into Alexandra Towing Co ownership, renamed *Wellington*. A year later she was sold to the Vernicos Shipping Co, Greece, becoming the *Vernicos Costas.*

Above: Seen secured in the entrance to the lock leading to the Gladstone Dock, the Rea Towing Co's *Grassgarth* (231grt, 103ft) was built in 1953 by A. Hall & Co, Aberdeen. The Rea tugs based at Avonmouth and Southampton, operated by R. & J. H. Rea Ltd, could be distinguished from their counterparts at Liverpool by their funnel colours. In place of the white-bordered black 'Cory' diamond (carrying the letter 'R') on the Liverpool tugs, they had a light blue 'Cory' diamond.

67

Below: Another Liverpool Screw Towing tug, the *Grebe Cock* (169grt, 101ft) in the Gladstone/ Hornby lock. Built by Cammell Laird in 1935, the *Grebe Cock* was converted to burn oil fuel in 1960. She remained on the Mersey until August 1967, when she was sold to Northern Slipways, Dublin. Just four months later she was sold again, for breaking-up at Troon.

In the background, beyond the lines of new Rootes Group cars, is the Liverpool Overhead Railway, which ran from Seaforth to Herculaneum Dock at an average height of 16ft above road level; opened in 1893, it closed in 1956.

Left: The *Grebe Cock* again, here heaving away under the bows of an unidentified ship.

Rea Towing, North West Tugs and Alexandra Towing tugs together in this typically busy Liverpool scene in the Kings Dock/Queens Dock area, just to the south of the Princes Landing Stage. The *Heath Cock* (193grt) was one of the earliest motor tugs to join the Liverpool Screw Towing/ North West Tugs fleet, delivered in 1958 by Cammell Laird & Co. The Rea tug (in the middle of the picture) is the *Rosegarth*, which, like the five other vessels of her class (*Applegarth*, *Aysgarth*, *Bangarth*, *Grassgarth* and *Throstlegarth*) — all-six built 1950-4 — has plated-in sides on her main deck, with her crew accommodation placed across the forward end of the enclosed structure. A disadvantage with this arrangement was that access between the aft deck spaces and the anchor deck, forward, could only be obtained by climbing up and over the boat deck.

The two ships in the picture are, on the left, the China Mutual Steam Navigation motorship *Atreus* of 7,800 tons gross, built in 1951 by Vickers Armstrong, and, to the right (beyond the three tugs), the 9,780grt steamship *Indian Resolve*, built in 1956 for the Indian Steamship Co, Calcutta, by Howaldtswerke AG, Hamburg. The latter was broken up at Bombay in 1978 after serving the same company throughout her life.

Another superb picture of a Mersey steam tug in action: the Alexandra Towing Co's *Hornby* (201grt, 103ft), ably assisted by the Johnston Warren Line's motor tug *Foylemore* (208grt). They are towing the Shaw Savill Line 10,674grt cargo/passenger liner *Doric* through the Gladstone/Hornby lock. The *Hornby*, completed in 1936 by Cochrane & Sons, Selby, was originally stationed at Southampton. While there, in April 1947, along with 17 other tugs, she was involved in towing the giant new Cunard liner *Queen Elizabeth* off the Brambles bank in the Solent, where she had grounded. (Of the other tugs engaged in the operation, the *Canute*, *Neptune* and *Sloyne* can be seen elsewhere in this book.)

The *Doric* and a sister ship, the *Delphic*, were the first postwar refrigerated motorships to be built for Shaw Savill's UK–Australia/ New Zealand cargo service. Introduced in July 1949, following construction by the Fairfield Shipbuilding & Engineering Co at Glasgow, the *Doric* was scrapped at Tamise, Belgium, in 1969 after a relatively short career. The *Hornby* was sold to North West Tugs in December 1966 and renamed *North Cock*; she was broken up at Dalmuir on the River Clyde in 1968.

Another of the large towage fleets at Liverpool and on the River Mersey, until absorbed by Alexandra Towing in 1968, was that of J. H. Lamey, whose tugs could be recognised by the prominent black 'L' they carried on the white band of their funnels. This is the *James Lamey* (260grt, 114ft 6in), acquired by the company in 1958 and built as the *Flying Eagle* for the Clyde Shipping Co by Bow, McLachlan & Co, Paisley, in 1928. Designed for coastal towing, she was provided with capacious bunkers. In her bows, mounted on a plate across the gunwale, she has a sturdy Samson post. The flying bridge was fitted for her new owners. The *James Lamey* worked extensively outside the bar at Liverpool, remaining with the Lamey fleet until purchased by Charles Brand Ltd for further employment at Belfast in 1966, when she was renamed *Lilias*. She was eventually broken up at Cork in 1969. Note the Mersey Docks & Harbour Board lettering on the building in the background.

The *John Lamey* (185grt, 100ft) (ex-*Geertruida XV*, ex-*Lady Elizabeth*) has been included as a good example of the converted steam tug, her modernised funnel shape being something of an indicator of the changes that have taken place within her. She was built with steam engines in 1927 by the Dutch shipbuilder Jonker & Stans at Hendrik-Ido-Ambacht but was partially re-engined with a diesel power-plant after joining the Lamey tug fleet in 1956. As such, she was the first motor tug in service on the River Mersey.

Behind the *John Lamey* can be seen the funnel of a Liverpool Screw Towing steam tug; berthed further back in this misty Birkenhead scene is a Shaw Savill or Bibby Line cargo/passenger liner. Perhaps the most famous landmark on the Liverpool waterfront, the Royal Liver Building (home of the Royal Liver Friendly Society), can just be discerned in the distance, to the right.

Later in her career, the *John Lamey* was renamed *Harry Sharman*, and it was under this name that she was wrecked below Culver Down, near Bembridge, Isle of Wight, in late October 1970 during efforts to assist the stricken oil tanker *Pacific Glory*, which had caught fire following a collision with another tanker, the *Allegro*.

A busy scene at the Birkenhead Docks as three Alexandra Towing Co steam tugs bustle around the 25,516grt, 640ft Canadian Pacific passenger mail liner *Empress of Britain*. Of the three tugs, the two nearest are the very similar *North Quay* (on the left) and *North End*. The *North Quay* (219grt, 104ft 6in) entered service in 1956, built by Scott & Sons, Bowling; like the *North End*, she was sold to Rimachiatori Sardi SpA in 1972, being renamed *Terralba*.

The *Empress of Britain*, paired with the *Empress of England*, served on the Liverpool–Montreal route until 1964, when the Greek Line acquired her and placed her on the Haifa/Piraeus–New York service as the *Queen Anna Maria*. Diverted to full-time cruising in 1976, she remains afloat, almost 40 years later, as the cruise ship *Topaz*, having in the interim been named *Olympic*, *Fiesta Marina* and *Carnivale*. As an interesting addendum, for many years Canadian Pacific operated three tender tugs of its own at Liverpool — the *Bison*, the *Moose* and the *Wapiti*.

Left: Three Liverpool Screw Towing steam tugs, among them the *Storm Cock* (169grt, 101ft), handling the 8,922grt Bibby liner *Leicestershire* in the Birkenhead Docks. The *Storm Cock* was constructed nearby, at the Cammell Laird & Co shipyard, in 1936. She was scrapped at Dalmuir 32 years later, in 1968. The *Leicestershire* maintained the Bibby Line's UK–Burma (Rangoon) route, carrying general cargo and 76 first-class passengers. She was built in 1949 by the Fairfield Shipbuilding & Engineering Co, Glasgow. In her later years, the *Leicestershire* became the Greek passenger/car ferry *Heraklion*, which was lost in tragic circumstances on 12 December 1966, barely two years after she had been purchased by Typaldos Line. Converted to carry 300 passengers and vehicles on the Piraeus–Crete route, she ran into a severe winter gale while returning to her home port. As huge waves pounded her, the poorly secured trucks and cars on the vehicle deck were shaken free. One of these, a refrigerated truck, smashed open a loading hatch, causing the ship to flood. Before aid could reach the stricken vessel, she foundered off Falconcra in the Cyclades Islands, with the loss of 241 lives.

The other large ship in this picture, berthed beyond the tugs, is the Pacific Steam Navigation Co's 17,872grt motor liner *Reina del Pacifico*. Launched by Harland & Wolff, Govan, on 23 September 1930, she commenced her maiden voyage from Liverpool to Valparaiso, Chile, the following April. The career of the *Reina del Pacifico* ended in 1958 when she was sold to be broken up at Newport, South Wales.

Right: Heading a line of berthed Liverpool Screw Towing tugs is the 1929-built *Thistle Cock* (169grt, 101ft), another of five similar tugs built by Cammell Laird, Birkenhead. The Liverpool Screw Towing & Lighterage Co was formed in 1877 and was among the first towage concerns to order screw-propelled tugs for deep-sea work in place of paddle vessels, although the majority of their new-buildings were swiftly taken up for Admiralty service. The company lost its identity in 1966 when it was absorbed into Alexandra Towing. As a result of the fleet rationalisation which followed, the *Thistle Cock* was disposed of a year later, being sold to the Northern Slipways Co, Dublin, but ultimately broken up at Troon within 12 months of the sale.

Left: Another pair of Rea Towing tugs, pictured in the Gladstone/ Hornby lock, the sister tugs *Throstlegarth*, nearest, and *Rosegarth* (both 231grt, 103ft). The last two of a group of six triple-expansion steam tugs built by A. Hall & Co, Aberdeen, they entered service in 1954. Like the *Grebe Cock* and *Thistle Cock*, the *Throstlegarth* ended her days at shipbreakers in Troon, having previously been sold to Northern Slipways, Dublin. The *Rosegarth*, with her sister *Applegarth*, was sold to the Holyhead Towing Co, North Wales, in September 1970. They were renamed, respectively, as the *Afon Wen* and *Afon Cefni*. Later, in February 1973, the pair were sold again, to Italian owners.

Above: The Rea tug *Throstlegarth* again, towing the China Mutual Steam Navigation Co's *Perseus* through the Gladstone lock. The 10,113grt *Perseus*, last of a group of four vessels for the Liverpool–Japan service, was a cargo/passenger motor ship completed by Vickers Armstrong in 1950, provided with accommodation for 31 first-class passengers. In 1967 she was reduced to a freighter, going to the breakers at Kaohsiung, Taiwan, six years later.

Left: The sister tugs *Wapping* and *Alfred* make a threesome of Alexandra Towing Co tugs with the postwar-built *North End*, just visible in the background of this bright Liverpool port scene. The *Wapping* and the *Alfred* (both 215grt, 103ft) were built by Cochrane & Sons, Selby, entering service, respectively, in 1936 and 1937. The *Wapping* was renamed *Marsh Cock* in January 1967 when she was sold to North West Tugs. She briefly rejoined the *Alfred* a year later, when they were broken up alongside each other at Dalmuir.

Right: The former Alexandra Towing tug *Sloyne* (300grt, 114ft), which spent much of her career stationed at Southampton, transferred to Belfast in 1966, having been purchased by Charles Brand Ltd as the *Lavinia*. As the *Sloyne*, she was completed in 1928 by J. Crichton & Co at Chester. The photograph was taken in July 1967, two years before she was broken up at Cork.

Below right: Another wartime-built 'Warrior'-class tug, the *Piper* (ex-*Empire Piper*) (250grt, 114ft 6in) wears the colours of John Cooper, the long-established Belfast towage concern. Constructed in 1942 by Clelands (Successors) Ltd at Wallsend-on-Tyne, the *Empire Piper* passed into civilian ownership in 1947. In the background of this June 1967 picture are two ships belonging to John Kelly & Co. That on the right is the motorship *Ballylesson* of 1,092 tons gross, built for this Belfast ship-owner in 1959 by A. Hall & Co, Aberdeen, along with a sister vessel, the *Ballyloran*.

Front cover: Operating on the River Thames at Gravesend near the Royal Terrace Pier, the William Watkins tug *Kenia* (200grt, 107ft), built in 1927 by Cochrane & Sons, Selby. She is a good example of the typical commercial steam tug, many of which were still operating in UK ports in the late 1950s, with steel hull, tall, slim funnel and open bridge. The *Kenia* was beached following a collision with the motor vessel *Maashaven* in 1964. Subsequently, she was withdrawn from service and sold. William Watkins, her owner, was the earliest of the commercial tug-operating companies on the Thames.

Back cover: Berthed in the Gladstone Dock, Liverpool, Alexandra Towing Co's *North End* (206grt, 104ft 6in), which was built in 1957 by W. J. Yarwood & Sons, Northwich. Her oil-fired steam engines had a power output of 1,050ihp (indicated horsepower). Beyond her is the small steam craft-handling tug *Redcroft* (56grt) owned by W. Bate & Co and dating from 1936. In 1972 the *North End* was sold to Rimachiatori Sardi SpA, Cagliari, which renamed her *Figari*.

Acknowledgements
John Barrett
Museum in Docklands (R. R. Aspinall)
Red Funnel Group
R. C. Riley
Royal Naval Museum Information Services (Mrs Allison Wareham)
Southampton Central Library — Maritime Collections
Philip N. Thomas
World Ship Society Central Record (J. V. Bartlett)

Bibliography

Bowen, Frank C.	*A Hundred Years of Towage* — History of William Watkins, 1833-1933 (company commemorative publication)
Chesterton, D. Ridley	*abc British Tugs* — 4th and 5th editions (Ian Allan)
Hallam, B.	*Blow Five* (Journal of Commerce, 1976)
Hannan, B.	*Fifty Years of Naval Tugs* (Maritime Books, *c*1980)
Harvey & Turrell	*Empire Tugs* (World Ship Society)
Le Fleming, H. M.	*abc British Tugs* — 1st, 2nd and 3rd editions (Ian Allan)
Stammers, M. K.	*Tugs and Towage* (Shire Publications)
Thomas, P. N.	*British Steam Tugs* (Waine Research Publications, 1983)

plus numerous issues of Lloyds Registers of Shipping and *Marine News* (the monthly magazine of the World Ship Society)

Left: The Port of London Authority owned a substantial fleet of its own tugs, comprising both ship-handling tugs and smaller, craft-handling river tugs for moving lighters. The twin-screw *Beam* (168grt, 91ft), one of the former type, dated from 1910. Built by Ferguson Bros at Port Glasgow, she is seen here at Tilbury with the Ellerman's City Line cargo-passenger ship *City of Colombo*. The latter, a motorship of 7,739 tons gross and measuring 507ft in overall length, entered service in 1956, having been built by Barclay, Curle & Co on the River Clyde; she was broken up at Kaohsiung, Taiwan, from February 1979, less than two years after being transferred to Ben Line Steamers as the *Benmohr*. Another Ellerman-group ship can be seen beyond her in this view.